Rewriting the Vietnam Narrative: Strategic Partnership Opportunities in Southeast Asia

A narrow space of time from 1959 thru 1975 during what the West calls the Vietnam War and the Vietnamese People refer to as the American War defines what many consider the US-Vietnam Narrative. The impact of this conflict on the international and domestic path of the United States and its future National Strategy cannot be understated nor the lessons learned forgotten. The scar on American prestige and soul continues to heal as do the wounds absorbed by the people of Vietnam. The bloody civil war they fought robbed South Vietnam of its sovereignty and cost North Vietnam dearly in lives to unify two separate Vietnams. While it certainly remains an important part of a shared history it doesn't define the future for an ancient civilization with the resilience of the Vietnamese people nor should it for that of the United States.

In 2011 the United States signaled to the world an unprecedented shift in strategic focus to the Pacific. The rebalancing of American National Power into a region devoid of the level of American Diplomacy, Information, Military, and Economic (DIME) resources applied to other regions of the world has forced the reset of regional strategic norms. This paper explores why it is in both the United States' and Vietnam's national interest to improve their cooperation and partnership. Understanding Vietnamese history, geography, and culture is critical to truly grasping the opportunity this emerging relationship presents to both nations. The core of this paper documents the coordinated application of the elements of National Power focusing predominantly on the military. This includes what has been implemented to date as well a strategy to enhance cooperation and stimulate meaningful engagement with Vietnam and conversely within the greater Southeast Asia Region.

Why build a trusting, enduring partnership with a Communist Vietnam? On the surface this appears to be a valid concern. In President Truman's "A Report to the National Security Council – NSC 68" on April 12th, 1950 a strategy to contain the spread of Communism established a doctrine followed by all administrations until the collapse of the Soviet Union in the 1990's.[1] Vietnam's Communist Government when viewed through the lens of historical United States policy and thought is conceivably an ideological adversary to freedom and should be contained and isolated much like Cuba and North Korea. After all, the United States expended great amounts of blood and treasure to fight the Communist in Vietnam from 1959-1975 only to see the Democratic Government in the South ultimately defeated by the Communist forces of North Vietnam. A marble wall in Washington with the names of 58,272 fallen U.S. Soldiers inscribed on it bears witness reminding all those that view it of the price paid in American blood to stop communism.[2] Also, in 1975 an initial wave of 125,000 Vietnamese refugees began to arrive in the United States fleeing victorious communist forces in Vietnam and paving the way for over a million more of their countrymen to follow.[3] Their ordeal and the risks they took to reach these shores underscored the fear the communist takeover represented.

Thirty eight years later and in light of the current regional issues in Southeast Asia, coupled with American interest in the region, it is important to craft a strategy that is nuanced and intuitive. Historically the United States has viewed countries practicing communist forms of government as potential adversaries posing a clear threat to democracy and our national security. Diplomatic dialogue by the U.S. State Department with the Soviet Union, North Korea, Cuba, Vietnam, and even China demonstrated a historically dysfunctional approach to cooperating and engaging forms of government dramatically different from that of the United States. In most cases diplomatic paralysis, embargoes, and in extreme cases direct and indirect military conflict replaced dialogue, engagement, and cooperation. The use of the pillars of U.S. National Power, namely diplomatic, informational, military, and economic policies demonstrated a strong acceptance that these potential enemies must be contained and weakened to a point that democracy could take hold. While the past fears of communist regional and world-wide expansion have failed to materialize, the essence of a single party system of Vietnam known as the Communist Party of Vietnam or the Dang Cong San Viet Nam still leads to valid concerns revolving around many areas grouped succinctly under the umbrella of human rights issues discussed later.

By expanding the view to the larger strategic picture of Southeast Asia today and its impact on the United States National Interest, it is easier to find there is more that attracts then separates. There are many reasons for the increasingly interwoven and interdependent relationship developing across the Pacific, but the primary catalyst driving these former enemies closer together is the increasing power, influence, and threat China poses to her smaller neighbors coupled with vital American economic interest in this region. While land border conflicts have erupted throughout Vietnam's long and auspicious history, the critical points of friction are currently territorial disputes within the South China Sea and the vast resources that lie beneath it.

Vietnam claims sovereignty over the Spratly and Paracel Islands. "It has claimed an exclusive economic zone (EEZ) of 200 nautical miles and the adjacent continental shelf in the South China Sea (East Sea—Bien Dong in Vietnamese) on the basis of natural prolongation.[4] Basing these claims on records and maps from pre-French colonial period documents, "Vietnam has increasingly been arguing in terms of modern international law—that is, the 1982 United Nations Convention on Law of the Sea (UNCLOS)—to substantiate its claims to EEZ and continental shelf areas in the South China Sea proper, the Gulf of Thailand, and the Gulf of Tonkin."[5] China also claims both archipelagos based on the South China Sea being its historical waters. In 1992, China officially claimed most of the South China Sea as Chinese territorial waters, which included the Paracel as well as the Spratly archipelagos and signed an energy exploration agreement with Crestone Energy Corporation.[6] Vietnam has also has been utilizing the UNCLOS to argue its territorial rights in the South China Sea including both archipelagos.[7]

In the United States "Pivot to the Pacific", one of the primary justifications is "China's growing military capabilities and its increasing assertiveness of claims to disputed maritime territory, with implications for freedom of navigation and the United States' ability to project power in the region."[8] This regional territorial dispute has strategic implications for the United States requiring a nuanced strategy to prevent escalation between both China and her neighbors. Maintaining the freedom of navigation through the South China Sea as well as the security and economic well being of the entire region are key national interest of the United States. It is in this 21st Century twist on Southeast Asian regional politics and thirst for resources that the old proverb "the enemy of my enemy is my friend" creates the opportunity for a strong East-West alliance to counter a growing Chinese power in the region.

In order to put the potential partnership between the United States and Vietnam into proper context one must first understand Vietnam's history to gain an appreciation for its current fears and concerns. The Vietnamese civilization officially came into existence in history under King An Duong in the third century BC. In 111 B.C. the Han dynasty invaded from China quickly conquering the Viet people. The Vietnamese continued to pursue their freedom in a short lived rebellion in 40 A.D. and later completely routed their Chinese occupiers in the tenth century at the battle of Bach Dang River where they employed an ancient version of the punji stake to sink the Chinese fleet and force the more powerful Chinese forces to leave their country. In line with their fighting techniques and skills honed over centuries of fighting vastly superior enemy forces they used smaller versions of this same weapon nearly a thousand years later with some effect against American foot soldiers. Fighting continued against the Cambodians, Mongols and even the Chinese again as they all invaded and were eventually defeated. The lessons learned by the Vietnamese people were enduring and proved their will, cohesion, and tactics could defeat military powers much greater than their own.[9]

In 1858 the French invaded Vietnam pulling much of Southeast Asia under their control by the 1880's. They subjected the people of Vietnam to their colonial policies remaining in tight control with the exception of World War II when Japan seized Vietnam and occupied it until the defeat of the Japanese Empire by the Allies in 1945 and the French re-occupied their former colonies. The French fought conventionally against

Communist forces utilizing guerrilla tactics under Ho Chi Minh and were defeated by in at the Battle of Dien Bien Phu on 7 May, 1954.[10] Later that year, a peace treaty forced France to divide the country between the Communist in the North and anti-Communist government in the South.

The United States began to provide military assistance and aid in the late 1950's when the Communist North attempted to gain control of the South and unify the country. This assistance gradually turned into the commitment of major U.S. ground forces and a large scale conflict ensued until an armistice ended the war and U.S. Military Forces departed Vietnam in 1973 at the cost of nearly 60,000 American lives and 111 billion dollars (738 billion dollars in today's money) as well as millions of Vietnamese lives.[11] The Vietnam War was not the end of conflict or loss for Vietnam.

Possibly a warning of the consequences of not addressing territorial disputes on 25 December 1978, Vietnam invaded Cambodia after repeated land and maritime clashes resulting in the fall of the Cambodian Khmer Rouge Government.[12] On 17 February 1979, Chinese forces attacked across the Northern border of Vietnam over a myriad of issues, primarily Vietnams close ties with the Soviet Union. The incursion known as the Third Indo-China War or the Sino-Vietnamese War lasted only 29 days, but resulted in roughly the same number of killed in action that the United States lost in over a decade of conflict in Vietnam. This also more importantly reinforced the reality that despite a shared political ideology, the growing dragon to the North that is China will always carry a sword unsheathed ready to strike its smaller neighbor to the South. This eternal threat increasingly shapes and drives Vietnamese diplomacy and strategy as Vietnam takes its place as a regional power.[13]

A map of Vietnam clearly illustrates why it is at the epicenter and ultimately the solution to the ongoing maritime territorial disputes in the South China Sea. Vietnam boosts a long and arguably strategic 3,444 kilometer coastline along the hotly contested South China Sea comprising a total land area of 325,360 Square Kilometers that shares borders with Cambodia, Laos, and China.[14] "A map of Vietnam describes an elongated S, swerving symmetrically along its southern sweep, tapering neatly through the midsection, but foreshortened and bulging to the north. Mountains form the spine of this 1,025-mile-long (1,650 km) country, roughly paralleling its borders with Cambodia and Laos. But rivers and the sea provide greater definition, both visually and culturally, along the 2,135-mile (3,444 km) seaboard and the two great waterways of the Mekong and Red Rivers."[15] Climate modeling exercises demonstrate Vietnam's vulnerability to the effects of Global Warming. Its long coastline comprised of low-lying coastal areas with high concentrations of population increase the impact of storms, rising sea levels and drought. Four Dams built in China with four more planned impact the flow of the Mekong River as well as nine additional dams in Cambodia and Laos.[16]

Understanding and embracing a people's culture is essential in building a strong partnership today especially when taken in the context of colonialism and conflict between the West and East. Lieutenant Colonel Ovidiu L. Uifaleanu from the Romanian Army described culture "as an operational code that is valid for an entire group of people."[17] Vietnam remains heavily influenced by its own path through history and dramatically by the invasion as well as occupation over long periods of time by other cultures to include the Chinese, Japanese, French, and arguably the United States. "In Vietnam today, you're apt to see ball caps on the heads of the middle-aged and berets on the heads of the old-timers, but make no mistake: Twenty years of American sway and one hundred years of the French are nothing next to the influence spawned by a thousand years of Chinese rule and cultural osmosis."[18] The Chinese impact on Vietnamese culture cannot be overstated nor the fierce sense of distrust of China and acceptance that it will again have to fight for its freedom, lessons learned from thousands of years of a painful and costly history. Throughout a painful and at times violent past, the Vietnamese culture is one of resilience and optimism. They are a people who believe in hard work, frugalness, and remembering the past, but hopeful for a prosperous future. This forward thinking and openness to new opportunities drives a progressive diplomacy with an Asian, yet nuanced Western approach to addressing grievances and threats within Southeast Asia and the world.

Diplomatic relations with Vietnam in recent years have been very successful. In 1989, President George H. Bush was encouraged by Vietnam's withdrawal after its invasion of Cambodia and initiated actions to improve relations with Hanoi. In 1991, the President provided a plan to normalize relations with Vietnam as well as opening an office in Hanoi to improve liaison with POW/MIA issues. The momentum continued into the Clinton Administration when the embargo was ended in 1994 and the process of normalization continued, capped off with a very successful visit by President Bill Clinton in 2000 to Ho Chi Minh City (the former capital of South Vietnam called Saigon prior to 1975). In December 2001 the United States-Vietnam Bilateral Trade Agreement went into effect providing conditional trade relations to Vietnam becoming permanent in December 2006. "During the Bush Administration, the United States and Vietnam dramatically upgraded diplomatic and strategic aspects of their relationship to the point where the two countries have all-but-normalized bilateral relations."[19] The strategic importance of Vietnam's membership in the Association of Southeast Asian Nations (ASEAN) of which the United States nor its strongest allies in the region are not (Australia and Japan) cannot be understated. "During the July ASEAN Regional Forum (ARF) meeting, Vietnamese and U.S. officials orchestrated a multilateral diplomatic push-back against perceived Chinese assertiveness in the South China Sea. In October, Vietnam then convened and secured U.S. attendance in the first-ever ASEAN Defense Ministers' Meeting + 8."[20] This allowed for Defense Secretary Gates to voice concerns over China's aggressive actions in the South China Sea. Shortly afterwards another first occurred when Vietnam allowed Secretary of State Clinton to attend the East Asia Summit (EAS) in Hanoi. Clearly Vietnam is opening doors and establishing opportunities for the United States to become increasingly involved and supportive in the region. The National Security Strategy states, "We are expanding our outreach to emerging nations, particularly those that can be models of regional success and stability, from the Americas to Africa to Southeast Asia."[21] It would appear that Vietnam has a similar litmus test for outreach and engagement of Western nations.

Many of the suggestions in this paper to strengthen cooperation and partnership with Vietnam are evolving daily and intersect multiple elements of National Power. There are several steps the United States can take to bolster our diplomatic engagement with Vietnam and the region. First, resolving the territorial disputes in the South China Sea fairly and equitably is a priority. Vietnam has been very modest in its request for diplomatic support from the United States on this issue. Indeed, Vietnam has taken the wise and calculating statesman approach by using its 2010 ASEAN chairmanship to form a multi-country negotiation forum which requires all nations within the disputed area to conduct negotiations in a multilateral setting opposite of China's preferred divide and conquer strategy. Vietnam's request to the United States is to do "more to emphasize, through language or actions, that all parties to the dispute should adhere to common principles, such as promoting transparency, adhering to the rule of law, refraining from undertaking unilateral actions, and committing to the freedom of the seas and navigation."[22] The United States needs to diplomatically work with Vietnam on an equitable agreement on compensation for Agent Orange used throughout the Vietnam War to strip the jungle of vegetation as well increasing funding and involvement in demining operations discussed later.

The United States and the American people are surprisingly popular within Vietnam so informational opportunities exist to maintain and improve an already positive view rather than have to establish or fix a broken perception. "Although Vietnam suffered an estimated five million dead in its war with the United States (more than one million combatants and four million civilians), there's no visible animosity toward America."[23] In response to the Pew Global Attitudes Research question "Please tell me if you have a very favorable, somewhat favorable, somewhat unfavorable, or very unfavorable opinion of the United States", 71% of Vietnamese people responded favorably in 2002.[24] This favorable view of the United States is an incentive for U.S. Foreign Assistance which grew from one million dollars a year in the 1990's to over 140 million dollars in FY2011. Economic assistance is largely medical as well as de-mining operations, human rights programs and dioxin site cleaning (Agent Orange), but not direct compensation. In addition to the foreign aid programs, an investment in educational exchange programs for an additional ten million dollars per year demonstrates a continued commitment to the Vietnamese people.[25]

The application of Military Power is often most effective when not used kinetically. After the Vietnam War the United States Military and the Vietnam People's Army have worked slowly and deliberately to re-build trust. In 2005 both countries entered into an International Military and Education and Training (IMET) agreement which provided Vietnamese officers the opportunity to attend English language training in the United States. The modification of the International Traffic in Arms Regulation with regards to Vietnam authorized the sale of non-lethal defense equipment to Vietnam. Both Foreign Military Sales (FMS) and Foreign Military Funding (FMF) are now available to Vietnam. This represented over $100 million dollars worth of equipment and services between 2007- 2010.[26] "In 2011, Vietnam's Ministry of Defense for the first time sent Vietnamese officers to U.S. staff colleges and other military institutions."[27] In June of 2013, Vietnamese Brigadier General Pham Thuan will receive his diploma from the United States Army War College as one of an elite group of International fellows selected and honored to attend that esteemed institution. More importantly, this day also marks an historical achievement in both U.S. and Vietnamese military and diplomatic cooperation as the first Vietnamese Officer ever graduates from the United States Army Senior Service College.

In a movement to avoid direct U.S. military intervention in the region the United States "has continued its policy of upgrading its defensive ties with and the capabilities of many Southeast Asian militaries, particularly with Vietnamese security forces."[28] The 21st Century reality of decreased military budgets coupled with avoidance of U.S.

casualties has given rise in support of the strategy of Building Partner Capacity (BPC) within the region. The art in this strategy is the evaluation, equipping, organization, training, and synchronization of multiple regional partners into a regional force that can shape regional issues when military force is required. Nuanced opportunities exist for increased cooperation and partnership within the military to military realm that present little to no threat to neighbors who might be otherwise concerned with U.S. Military presence in the region. The United States Army National Guard's State Partnership Program's vision is to "establish and sustain enduring relationships with partner nations of strategic value in conjunction with the National Security Strategy, National Military Strategy, Department of State, and Combatant Command Theater Security Cooperation guidance to promote national objectives, stability, partner capacity, better understanding, and trust."[29] It is an extremely successful program of 65 global partnerships spanning all Combatant Commands. A partnership between Vietnam and a specific state National Guard Command would be coordinated through the Combatant Commander as well as the U.S. Ambassador's country team to ensure effects tailored to meet the specific U.S. and Vietnamese objectives.

The Guard Soldiers and assets are available to provide a myriad of support and training opportunities from medical support, disaster relief, homeland defense/security, and training/exercise opportunities from small unit to large scale training opportunities such as Cobra Gold in Thailand. Other areas of concern that these forces could provide technical and/or hands on support are border/port security which could assist in mitigating some Vietnamese-Chinese tension as well as demining operations.[30] Demining is an extremely important issue in Vietnam. An estimated that 3.5 million

12

mines as well as 300,000 tons of unexploded ordinance remain within Vietnam from multiple conflicts. These weapons account for approximately 2,000 civilian casualties each year.[31] While these are a form of military power they also deliver a positive informational effect to the Vietnamese People and Government demonstrating in actions, not words, that American Soldiers are committed to the health and safety of our partners.

With the conclusion of the Vietnam war 1,971 Americans were unaccounted for. As of 1 August, 2012 with the assistance and support of Vietnam, 689 of those have been located and identified with another 597 listed as "no further pursuit" meaning it has been determined they were killed and no remains can be recovered. This represents the closure of 65% of these cases. These recovery missions marked the first milestone in United States/Vietnam military to military cooperation. Beyond the closure this brings to American families, it also represents a willingness on the part of Vietnam to help bring closure to this nation. These highly successful and rewarding missions are continuing with military teams deploying regularly now. There are four Joint Field Activities planned for FY13 supported by 95 U.S. and Vietnamese personnel lasting 30 days each.[32] Beyond this, the United States has an opportunity to provide teams and assistance to Vietnam to account, locate, and re-patriate MIA Vietnamese Soldiers and civilians. Currently there are hundreds of thousands of Vietnamese listed as missing during the war. In 2010, United States Agency for International Development (USAID) initiated a two-year program providing one million dollars per year to assist Vietnam with locating these remains, but that financial support as well as direct U.S. military and civilian support needs to be increased dramatically to clearly demonstrate our commitment to respect Vietnam's fallen as well as to help bring the same closure to countless Vietnamese families and a nation.[33] Military to Military professional education exchanges need investment in funding and talent management. They should reflect the same level of support and importance as those shared with traditional allies such as England and Australia. Discussion between military planners on how best to synchronize military assets and expertise for joint operations to combat the ever growing threat of piracy is another area for shared security and cooperation.

Vietnam's economic development has been impressive. "On his visit to the United States in 2005 –the first by a leader of communist Vietnam—Prime Minister Phan Van Khai rang the opening bell of the New York Stock Exchange, as symbolic a break from command economics as you're likely to get. Call it capitalist communism or communist capitalism."[34] Virtually non-existent before the embargo ended in 1994, trade between the United States and Vietnam in 2010 accounted for 18% of Vietnam's total exports. Import/export activity between both nations has grown from 222 million in 1994 to over 17 Billion in 2011.[35] "Vietnam's rapid economic transformation and global integration has lifted millions out of poverty and has propelled the country in the ranks of the lower-middle-income status."[36] The rapid rise of Vietnamese industry adds it to a powerful group of emerging regional trade partners in Southeast Asia tied closer to the United States with every container of goods exported to North American shores.

Vietnam is the world's second largest exporter of rice and second largest producer of coffee. It also produces a large part of the worlds clothing market resulting in a drop in their poverty level from 58% in 1992 to less than 30% in 2002.[37] Economically, Vietnam's success remains tied to the United States who represents the largest source of foreign investment and a growing trade partner. Current U.S. Policy on assistance to Vietnam "will focus on consolidating gains to ensure sustainable economic development and on promoting good governance and rule of law."[38] This assistance, synchronized with incentives for U.S. companies to continue to expand both import and export trade between our countries ensures continued economic growth. China still represents a major competitor in the region because it dominates the share of economic trade between the two nations. By investing in our trade relationship with Vietnam, both countries also become increasingly close economically. This in turn builds cohesive partnerships and familiarity within the intergovernmental arena, business world and more importantly within both populations.

Opportunities exist to strengthen our economic partnership and cooperation with Vietnam beyond financial investment. The territorial disputes in the South China Sea demonstrate there are substantial requirements for energy in the region. Assistance with the development of a nuclear energy program and infrastructure would provide Vietnam with vital electric energy providing stability and support for its growing economy. American companies represent the largest group of investors in Vietnam's industry at a time when more than half of Vietnam's population is under 25 and employment is extremely important. Encouragement of this continued American investment through incentives by both the United States and Vietnamese Governments could help ensure that a ready and willing workforce for American companies is available while the Vietnamese Government can benefit from low unemployment rates. American - Vietnamese partnership in the exploration and trade of natural resources provides an avenue for great economic and infrastructure investment. President

Barrack Obama has voiced his support for Vietnam's inclusion in the Trans Pacific Strategic Economic partnership. This along with granting Vietnam Generalized System of Preference (GSP) status, a free trade agreement (FTA) and bilateral investment treaty (BIT) will complete the strong economic foundation critical for a long lasting and mutually supportive partnership.

The United States can also send an important message by increasing cooperation and assistance in combating malnutrition. "The World Bank in 2005 estimated that about one-third of Vietnamese children under five years of age suffered from malnutrition."[39] An economic tool to assist in building this relationship is the USAID. The USAID "is the lead agency for the U.S. Government providing economic development and humanitarian assistance to people around the world."[40] Total projected foreign assistance to Vietnam will top 103 million dollars in 2013.[41]

It is wise not to completely ignore those that advocate caution in the continued strengthening of this partnership. Human rights continue to be the primary concern with the Vietnamese government. Freedom of the press and internet are tightly controlled and monitored. Persons charged with violating article 88 (propaganda against the government) can face up to 20 years in prison. Movements soon will include the requirement to use ones real name on the internet when blogging for instance and data servers are required to re-locate to local offices to allow for easy governmental control.[42] Another human rights issue in Vietnam is Human Trafficking for forced labor and commercial sexual exploitation. "State-owned and private labor export companies send tens of thousands of Vietnamese construction, fishing, and manufacturing workers overseas, where many are vulnerable to abuse and/or exploitation."[43]

Another factor in this calculation is the 1,548,449 Vietnamese Americans identified in the 2010 United States Census. Asians identifying themselves as Vietnamese Americans represent the fourth largest Asian population group in the United States. The group grew at a rate of 37.9% since the previous 2000 census comprised largely from refugees that fled Vietnam at the fall of Saigon as well as those that have journeyed and sought citizenship as diplomatic relations thawed.[44] The message from this group is from the individual perspective and collective groups depending upon the circumstances that drove them from Vietnam's shores, there remains a collective cautiousness, fear and in some cases, hatred for the political system that many believe robbed them of their homeland and birthright. This internal nation of Vietnamese Americans will be the most skeptical critics of this developing relationship, but also a key component to its long-term success.

Considering this and applying proper context, one cannot ignore the significant steps the government of Vietnam has taken to improve in other areas of Human Rights. Vietnam began to take meaningful steps to address Issues dealing with workers rights when it sought to improve internal economic conditions and engage in international trade. Workers in Vietnam now have the right to be a member of a union and based on Vietnamese labor codes, factories are required to have unions. In 2006 the U.S. State Department acknowledged "because of "many positive steps" taken by the Vietnamese government since 2004, the country was no longer a "severe violator of religious freedom" and was removed from the CPC (country of particular concern) list.[45] While there are still concerns about human rights abuses between the Vietnamese government and several minority groups to include the Kinh, Montagnards, Khmer, and

Hmong, there has been little conflict recently indicating improvement in cooperation and mutual understanding. This expressed willingness to adopt and implement internationally accepted norms by the government of Vietnam clearly demonstrates a progressive and Western-Friendly path.

The United States and Vietnam have a cultural openness and ability to overcome past conflict and cooperate towards a common future supported by mutually aligned national interest. Ironically, after centuries of resisting Western colonialism and influence, Southeast Asia acknowledges it requires the power and influence of a Western nation like the United States to counter a growing threat that China possibly possesses. On the other hand the United States cannot counter China's growing power and influence without the support and partnership of the smaller none the less strategically important countries that make up the region. The key is that this time both the West and the East have the opportunity to establish a positive and mutually beneficial partnership in which Vietnam can and should play a pivotal role. As nations within the region continue to take the lead on resolving territorial disputes within the South China Sea as well as ensuring maritime security and freedom of navigation, the world waits and watches. The United States and Vietnam cannot miss this opportunity to rewrite their shared narrative penned between 1959 to1975.

Endnotes

[1] http://www.trumanlibrary.org/whistlestop/study_collections/coldwar/documents/pdf/10-1.pdf

[2] "The Wall" linked from the Vietnam War Memorial Homepage at http://thewall-usa.com/information.asp (accessed December 22, 2012).

[3] "The History of Vietnamese Immigration" linked from the American Immigration Law Foundation Homepage at http://www.ailf.org/awards/benefit2005/vietnamese_essay.shtml (accessed December 22, 2012).

[4] Nguyen Hong Thao and Ramses Amer, "Managing Vietnam's Maritime Boundary Disputes," *Ocean Development & International Law* 38, no. 3 (August 2007): 306

[5] Ibid., 306.

[6] Ramses Amer, "The Territorial Disputes between China and Vietnam and Regional Stability," *Contemporary Southeast Asia* 19, no. 1 (June 1997): 88.

[7] Nguyen Ibid., 307.

[8] Mark E. Manyin, *Pivot to the Pacific? The Obama Administration's "Rebalancing" Toward Asia* (Washington, DC: Library of Congress, Congressional Research Service, March 28, 2012), 2.

[9] James Sullivan, *National Geographic Vietnam* (Washington, DC: National Geographic Society, 2006), 34-37.

[10] Bernard B. Fall, *Street Without Joy* (Mechanicsburg, PA: Stackpole Books, 1994), 328.

[11] Steven Daggett, *Cost of Major U.S. Wars* (Washington, DC: Library of Congress, Congressional Research Service, June 29, 2010), 1.

[12] "Country Studies: Cambodia" linked from the *Federal Research Division* at http://lcweb2.loc.gov/cgi-bin/query/r?frd/cstdy:@field(DOCID+kh0164) (accessed January 12, 2013).

[13] "Country Studies: Vietnam" linked from the *Federal Research Division* at http://lcweb2.loc.gov/cgi-bin/query/r?frd/cstdy:@field(DOCID+vn0129) (accessed January 12, 2013).

[14] "Vietnam: 2012 Country Review" linked from Country Watch at http://www.countrywatch.com.ezproxy.usawcpubs.org/cw_topic.aspx?type=text&vcountry=187&topic=PCPRF (accessed December 4, 2012)

[15] Sullivan, *National Geographic Vietnam*, 24.

[16] Mark E. Manyin, *U.S.-Vietnam Relations in 2011: Current Issues and Implications for U.S. Policy* (Washington, DC: Library of Congress, Congressional Research Service, May 18, 2012), 30.

[17] Lieutenant Colonel Ovidiu L. Uifaleanu, "NATO's Comprehensive Approach – A Challenge for Cultural Training, USAWC SRP, and (19 March 2010): 13.

[18] Sullivan, *National Geographic Vietnam*, 28.

[19] Manyin, *U.S.-Vietnam Relations in 2011: Current Issues and Implications for U.S. Policy*, 4-5.

[20] Ibid., 6.

[21] Barrack H. Obama, National Security Strategy (Washington, D.C.: The White House, May 2010), 3.

[22] Manyin, *U.S.-Vietnam Relations in 2011: Current Issues and Implications for U.S. Policy*, 6.

[23] Sullivan, *National Geographic Vietnam*, 12.

[24] "Global Attitudes Project" Linked from the Pew Research Center Homepage at http://www.pewglobal.org/database/?indicator=1&survey=1&response=Favorable&mode=chart (accessed December 20, 2012).

[25] Manyin, *U.S.-Vietnam Relations in 2011: Current Issues and Implications for U.S. Policy*, 13.

[26] Ibid., 21.

[27] Ibid., 20.

[28] Ibid., 7.

[29] "The National Guard State Partnership Program" linked from the National Guard Homepage at http://www.nationalguard.mil/features/spp/default.aspx (accessed December 19, 2012).

[30] Ibid.

[31] Bill Clinton, "Remarks on Demining in Hanoi, Vietnam", Hanoi, Vietnam, November 18, 2000.

[32] "Vietnam War" linked from the DPMO Defense Prisoner of War – Military Missing in Action Office Homepage at http://www.dtic.mil/dpmo/vietnam/ (accessed December 20, 2012).

[33] Manyin, *U.S.-Vietnam Relations in 2011: Current Issues and Implications for U.S. Policy*, 24.

[34] Sullivan, *National Geographic Vietnam*, 10.

[35] Manyin, *U.S.-Vietnam Relations in 2011: Current Issues and Implications for U.S. Policy*, 10.

[36] "Vietnam" linked from Foreignassistance.gov Homepage at http://www.foreignassistance.gov/OU.aspx?OUID=199&FY=2013&AgencyID=0 (accessed December 12, 2012).

[37] Manyin, *U.S.-Vietnam Relations in 2011: Current Issues and Implications for U.S. Policy*, 25.

[38] Ibid., 10.

[39] Ibid., 26.

[40] "Vietnam" linked from the USAID Homepage at http://vietnam.usaid.gov/FAQ (accessed December 27, 2012).

[41] "Vietnam" linked from Foreignassistance.gov Homepage at http://www.foreignassistance.gov/OU.aspx?OUID=199&FY=2013&AgencyID=0 (accessed December 12, 2012).

[42] Manyin, *U.S.-Vietnam Relations in 2011: Current Issues and Implications for U.S. Policy*, 15.

[43] Ibid., 19.

[44] "The Vietnamese Population of the United States: 2010" linked from the U.S. Census Homepage at http://www.bpsos.org/mainsite/images/DelawareValley/community_profile/us.census.2010.the%20vietnamese%20population_july%202.2011.pdf (accessed February 7, 2013).

[45] Manyin, *U.S.-Vietnam Relations in 2011: Current Issues and Implications for U.S. Policy*, 17-18.

Page Intentionally Left Blank

Page Intentionally Left Blank